John Franco

by Mark Stewart

ACKNOWLEDGMENTS

The editors wish to thank John Franco for his cooperation in preparing this book.
Thanks also to Integrated Sports International for their assistance.

PHOTO CREDITS

All photos courtesy AP/Wide World Photos, Inc. except the following:

Rob Tringali, Jr./Sports Chrome – Cover, 5 bottom right, 8, 23 top right, 27, 29, 33 right,
        46 bottom right, 47 bottom right
Sports Chrome – 5 top, 6, 21, 33 left
Brian Doyle/Sports Chrome – 24
St. John's University – 12, 22 top left
B&L Photographers – 17
Indianapolis Indians – 18
Steve Greico – 19, 22 bottom left
Mark Levine – 37
Mark Stewart – 48

STAFF

Project Coordinator: John Sammis, Cronopio Publishing
Series Design Concept: The Sloan Group
Design and Electronic Page Makeup: Jaffe Enterprises, and
        Digital Communications Services, Inc.

LIBRARY OF CONGRESS CATALOGING-IN-PUBLICATION DATA

Stewart, Mark.
    John Franco / by Mark Stewart.
        p. cm. – (Grolier all-pro biographies)
    Includes index.
    Summary: A brief biography of the All-Star relief pitcher of the New York Mets.
    ISBN 0-516-20172-7 (lib. bdg.) – 0-516-26020-0 (pbk.)
    1. Franco, John, 1960-   –Juvenile literature. 2. Baseball players–United States–
Biography– Juvenile literature. 3. Pitchers (Baseball)–United States–Biography–Juvenile
literature. [1. Franco,   John, 1960-   . 2. Baseball players.] I. Title. II. Series.
    GV865.F65S84 1996
    796.357'092–dc20
    [B]   96-12175
                                                                                          CIP
                                                                                           AC

Grolier ALL-PRO Biographies™

John Franco

by
Mark Stewart

CHILDREN'S PRESS®
A Division of Grolier Publishing
New York • London • Hong Kong • Sydney
Danbury, Connecticut

Contents

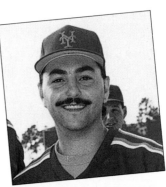

Who

Am I?

Someone once said that you can take a boy out of Brooklyn, but you can never take Brooklyn out of a boy. That describes me pretty well. I have played baseball in Florida, New Mexico, Texas, Indiana, Kansas, and Ohio, but my Brooklyn accent always gave me away. The moment I open my mouth, people always know where I am from. My name is John Franco, and this is my story . . . "

"Someone once said that you can take a boy out of Brooklyn, but you can never take Brooklyn out of a boy."

Growing Up

John Franco grew up in the Bensonhurst section of Brooklyn, New York. His family lived in a small apartment that was part of the Marlboro Housing Projects. There John learned how to play all sorts of baseball games, including wiffle ball, stickball, and stoopball. He and his older brother, Jim, shared the same bedroom and also shared a love of sports. In their games, Jim

John learned early that being a good relief pitcher means having to give something extra.

Tug McGraw was John's favorite Met.

would let John get way ahead, and then come back to beat him. This drove John crazy, but it also taught him how to save a little extra for the end of a game—the perfect training for a major-league relief pitcher. In fact, John credits Jim with making him a great "closer."

John and the other children who lived in the Marlboro Projects were always playing sports. They would pretend to be famous New York athletes, such as Tom Seaver, Brad Park, Walt Frazier, and Joe Pepitone. John's favorite player was Tug McGraw, the star reliever for the New York Mets. John went to Mets games whenever he could, and watched the team on television. His dream was to ride on the "Mr. Met" bullpen car. Unlike many other kids in their neighborhood, John and his friends did not experiment with drugs and alcohol, and they did not steal. They got their thrills from throwing a touchdown pass, making a long jump shot, or hitting a home run.

Although he liked sports more than schoolwork, John was still a good student. His favorite subject was social studies. John liked to imagine what it was like living in the United States when it was still a young country. He also enjoyed reading about American Indian cultures, U.S. presidents, and explorers such as Christopher Columbus.

"There is nothing more important than learning how to read," says John. "That's why, if you are having problems, there's so many people out there who can help you read, write, spell, whatever you want to do. Without knowing how to read, it will not only be hard to get through this society, but you will be locked out of a world that everyone else has access to."

John did not like all of his classes, but he realized how important it was to always pay attention to what the teacher was saying. That came in very handy in high school, when kids were not allowed to play on sports teams unless they maintained a good grade average.

John attended Lafayette High School, which was right across the street from the Marlboro Projects. It was exciting to play for the school's baseball team, because Sandy Koufax had been a baseball and basketball star there 20 years earlier. Koufax went on to have an amazing career for the Brooklyn and Los Angeles Dodgers and ended up in the Hall of Fame. By the time John was a senior, a lot of people were predicting he might be a major leaguer,

Hall-of-Famer
Sandy Koufax attended
John's high school.

too. In his final season on the team, his record was 14–1, and he regularly struck out more than half the batters he faced. But when the major-league draft was held in the spring of 1979, John was not among those selected. At 5' 7" and only 140 pounds, he was considered too small to be a star. "Too short," John remembers. "They kept telling me I was too short."

St. John's University disagreed. The school offered him a scholarship, and John gladly accepted.

College

John Franco lived just a few miles from St. John's University, yet there was no easy way to get there. Going from Brooklyn to Queens may look easy on a map, but it took John nearly two hours of subway and bus rides to complete the trip. Still, the thought of getting a free education and a chance to prove all those pro baseball scouts wrong made the trip well worth the time and trouble it took.

John and another freshman pitcher, Frank Viola, became very close friends. They were a perfect match: John was a wise-cracking practical joker, and Frank loved to laugh. The two young hurlers also

Not drafted out of high school, John decided to attend St. John's University.

Years

became the stars of the St. John's team (then called the Redmen, now called the Red Storm). John and Frank combined to win 13 games and lose only two. That was a big relief for coach Joe Russo, who was very worried when Steve Bingham and Ron Kiene—the two players who anchored the pitching staff the year before—had poor seasons. John finished the year with a 2.25 ERA, pitching both as a starter and a reliever.

Eleven years after they teamed up at St. John's, Frank Viola and John were both New York Mets.

Over the next two seasons, John developed into a major-league prospect. He stopped trying to blow batters away and concentrated instead on getting them to hit his pitch. His best pitch was a twisting, diving ball that broke down and away from right-handed batters. The only drawback to this delivery was that it sometimes strained John's young arm. When St. John's made the College World Series in 1981, John was on the bench with a sore elbow. This made him very sad. It also made him realize that he had to take care of his arm. He dedicated himself to good health and training, and he did not suffer another elbow injury for 11 years.

After his junior year, John wondered if he would be selected in the major-league draft. His stats were good—and he had grown three inches while attending St. John's—but he feared that his arm problems might scare away the scouts. He did have one more year left with the Redmen, but he felt he was ready to be a professional. On draft day, John was a nervous wreck. What relief he felt when he got the news: he had been selected by the Los Angeles Dodgers in the fifth round.

John posted outstanding pitching stats in his three years at St. John's:

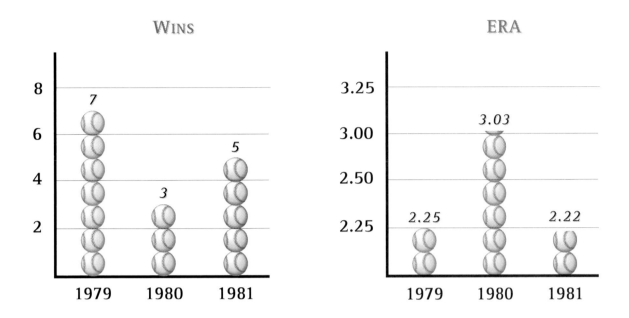

Being drafted by the Dodgers was a special moment. "Since I was a little kid, I wanted to be a baseball player. When the Dodgers called to tell me I was drafted, I was relieved. I had been on pins and needles all day. I was really happy they had picked me, because Sandy Koufax was one of my idols."

The Story

In the spring of 1981, the Dodgers sent John Franco to its minor-league team in Vero Beach, Florida, handed him the ball, and told him to do his thing. Although John now stood 5'10" and weighed 170 pounds, Dodger management was still not convinced he was big enough to be a dominant starter. Yet in just two years, John compiled an 18–11 record and jumped from L.A.'s lowest minor-league team to its highest team in AAA.

When the 1983 season started, the Dodgers knew they had a valuable pitcher in John Franco. Unfortunately, there was no room for John in the team's major-league starting rotation, and there were several more promising pitchers waiting for a chance. Los Angeles decided to trade him for what they really needed that season: a speedy player who could fill in at a number of different positions. When the Cincinnati Reds offered veteran Rafael Landestoy, the deal was done, and John reported to

Continues

Before reaching the major leagues, John pitched for the Indianapolis Indians, a Cincinnati Reds farm team.

his new team's AAA affiliate in Indianapolis, Indiana. It would be his last season as a starter.

In 1984, the Reds decided John would make a good relief pitcher. He had an excellent fastball, and he was a tough and aggressive competitor. He also had a strange pitch that looked like a fastball until it reached home plate. Then it would dip sharply to the left. It was a very hard pitch for batters to resist—especially the first time they saw it— and the result was often a weak grounder. Because relievers are

John spent only a short time in Indianapolis, but he was a fan favorite.

usually asked to come into a game and just get a few batters out, it made sense to move John into the bullpen. After a brief stay in the minors, John was promoted to the big leagues.

At first, it looked as if the Reds had pulled off the steal of the century in trading for John. John held opponents to eight hits in his first nine appearances, winning two games. But then he got clobbered for seven runs in his next eight innings, and the Cincinnati fans wondered if he was merely a "flash in the

pan." They got their answer when John bore down and did not allow a run in the next 13 games. Over the next five years, John saved 144 games, including 39 in 1988. That year he led the National League in saves and broke the team record of 37 set in 1972 by Clay Carroll. He was also named Fireman of the Year as top reliever in the league.

In December 1989, Franco got some exciting news. He had been traded back home to the New York Mets for reliever Randy Myers. In New York, John continued pitching brilliantly, notching a league-high 33 saves for the Mets and making the All-Star team for the fourth time

When John got to Cincinnati, fans wondered if he was a "flash in the pan."

in five seasons. After earning 30 more saves in 1991, some fans believed he was the best left-handed reliever in history. There was even talk of John making the Hall of Fame. If he could keep mowing down batters for another five or six years, he would stand a great chance of joining baseball's immortals in Cooperstown, New York.

In his third season with the Mets, John suffered the first serious injury of his professional career. The elbow problems that had haunted him way back in college had returned, and he spent much of the season simply trying to throw without pain. After a fabulous start, John had to go on the disabled list, and he finished the year with just 15 saves. In 1993, things only got

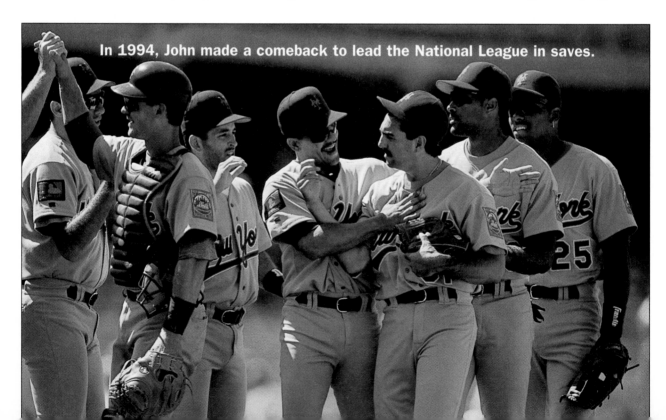

In 1994, John made a comeback to lead the National League in saves.

By 1996, John had the third most saves in baseball history.

worse, as he saved just 10 games. Was John's marvelous career over? Many baseball experts thought it was, but John worked hard to get back into shape. In 1994, he was the comeback story of the year in New York. He saved 30 games to lead all National League relievers. And just to prove he had returned to superstar status, John saved 29 games in 1995 to finish among the league leaders once again.

Does John still have a shot at the Hall of Fame? He most certainly does. He has saved more games than any left-hander who has ever played. That is not bad for a guy no one wanted when he began his career!

Timeline

1979: Joins St. John's Redmen

1988:
Records
career-
best 1.57
ERA and
leads NL
in saves

1990:
Leads
NL in saves
after trade
to New
York Mets

1984:
Becomes
full-time
closer for
Cincinnati
Reds

1994:
Wins
third
Fireman
of the
Year
award

1992: Elbow
injury cuts
short best
season of
his career

1996:
Records
300th
career
save

Game

John loves pitching before a crowd, even if he's on the road.

Action!

I like it on the road more because the crowd is against you. When you get out of an inning, 40,000 people are going home saying, 'If it wasn't for Franco, we would have won that game.'"

John enjoys being a relief ace because he gets to pitch almost every day. "Wouldn't I rather be a starter? No way! You have to wait five days to get back as a starter."

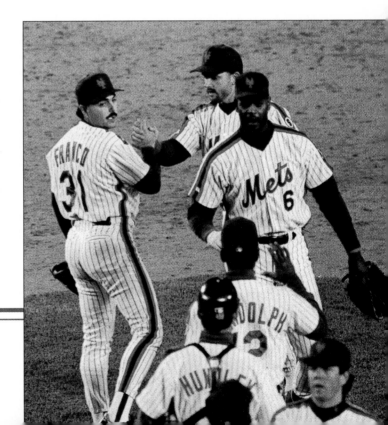

One of the first coaches John worked with in the Dodger organization was fellow Lafayette High graduate Sandy Koufax.

Did John begin his career expecting to be an All-Star? "Heck, I just wanted to make the big leagues. Anything else was icing on the cake."

John was sensational in his first season with the Mets. During one stretch, he saved nine games in nine appearances. He then went on the convert his next eight save opportunities.

As relief ace, the pitching staff relies on John to save the day.

Before John won the stopper's role in Cincinnati, he was one of baseball's top middle relievers.

People frequently ask John if his uniform number has some special meaning. "My answer is no, not really. That's just the uniform number that they gave me when I got called up to the big leagues. If the Reds had given me number 99 or number 0, I would have taken it, as long as I got to the major leagues. It's really not the number that's important, it's the person inside the uniform."

I pride myself on having been consistent all through my career. My goal is to maintain that consistency as long as I'm playing."

The first thing I had to learn when I came to the big leagues was how to keep my mouth shut. Sometimes you get in trouble with the media when you talk too much!"

John reacts after a blown save. He has learned to take the bad with the good.

Statistics show that left-handed hitters have pretty good success against John. What the numbers do not reveal is that only the league's very best lefties are allowed to hit against him. Everyone else gets pulled for a right-handed pinch hitter.

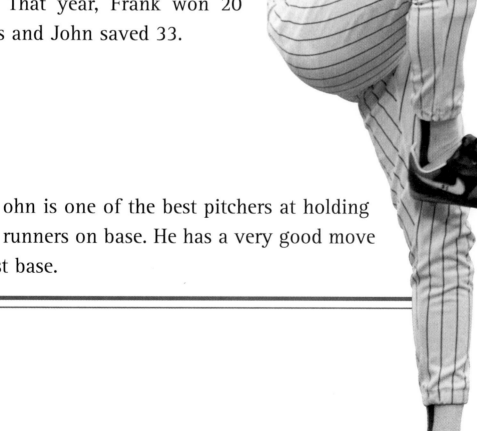

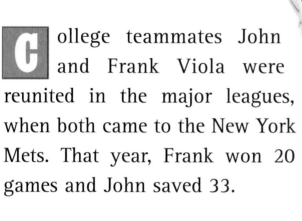College teammates John and Frank Viola were reunited in the major leagues, when both came to the New York Mets. That year, Frank won 20 games and John saved 33.

John is one of the best pitchers at holding runners on base. He has a very good move to first base.

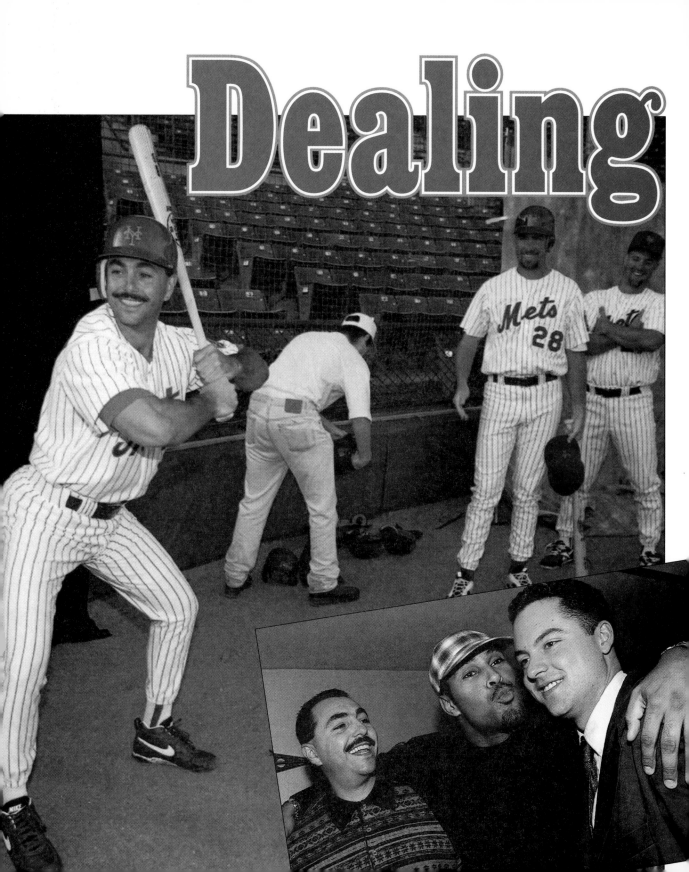

Dealing

With It

T he tension in a major-league clubhouse can tear a team apart—especially when things are not going well on the field. John Franco deals with this situation by goofing around, and playing practical jokes on teammates to break up the tension. John likes to remind his teammates that baseball is a hard game to play when you forget how to have fun.

"Basically, I see my job as someone who stays in the background and keeps the other guys loose. Of course, you have to know just how far you can go without hurting someone's feelings."

John makes believe he's a hitter at a spring training photo session. Inset: John keeps things loose with Mets teammates Ryan Thompson (center) and Rico Brogna (right).

HOW DOES

Unlike most successful relievers, John Franco does not possess an overpowering fastball. Although he gets his share of strikeouts, he prefers to shut down opposing hitters by making them hit into easy outs. As John sees it, this has been one of the keys to his long career.

"I'd rather throw three pitches and get a pop-up and two grounders than taking six pitches to strike out one guy. That way I reduce the strain on my arm, and I can pitch the next day if the team needs me."

John's delivery lets him throw a ball that breaks down and to the left.

He Do It?

The Grind

John Franco has one of the most nerve-racking jobs in baseball. Every time he is called to the mound, the game is on the line. Most of the time he comes through, but sometimes the other team beats him. And then he feels like he let the whole team down. One reason that John has been so successful for so many years is that he has learned to accept the ups and downs of his profession. But it has not been easy!

John says, "The hardest thing about what I do is maintaining an 'even keel.' That means understanding your limitations, and not trying to do too much. To maintain the same level year in and year out is a big challenge, but you have to be able to do it or you won't earn the respect of your opponents, and you will lose the confidence of your teammates."

John is constantly encouraging his teammates and keeping them loose.

Family

John and Rose Franco met in a Brooklyn disco when he was 17 and she was 15. They were married in 1986 and have two children, Nicole and John Jr., whom they call "J. J."

"My kids are starting to realize that their daddy is a professional baseball player, and they like coming to the ballpark and watching me perform on the field."

John and his parents, Jim and Mary, were extremely close. In fact, John considered his father his best friend. They were heartbroken when Mary lost her long battle with cancer and passed away in 1986. John purchased the house the family had been renting since moving from the projects in 1982, and moved in with his father. Sadly, Jim Franco suffered a heart attack on the job just 18 months later. John was devastated. His father had never been sick a day in his life. To honor him, John wore his orange Department of Sanitation T-shirt under his uniform.

John says, "My parents will always be with me."

Matters

Say What?

Here's what baseball people are saying about John Franco:

"John Franco is the best of the best."
—*Pete Rose, baseball great*

"He'll do anything to get people to laugh."
—*Frank Viola,
   former St. John's and Mets teammate*

"He's one of the best in the game, and yet can stay normal and treat people like people."

—*Bob Ojeda, former Mets teammate*

"You don't see left-handers throw strikes with off-speed pitches the way Franco does. Even when he gets behind in the count, he comes in with a change-up for a strike."

—*Bo Diaz, former All-Star catcher*

"John was tough, hard-nosed—a streetwise kid from Brooklyn. He'd kill you for a win."

—*Joe Russo, former St. John's coach*

"He is so funny. . . . If you've got problems, he won't let you think of them. He'll do something and you'll break up. I don't think people outside the game realize how important that is."

—*Howard Johnson, former Mets teammate*

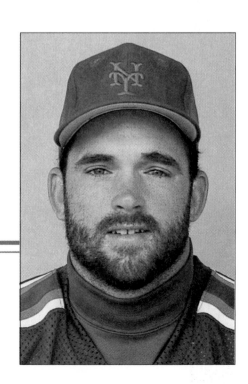

Career

If baseball ever invents a special award for the most valuable player off the field, John Franco would be the hands-down winner. He knows how to fire up his teammates, and he also knows when to keep them laughing. On the mound, John remains one of the most respected closers in the game. As long as he is used in a short relief role, he should continue to rack up saves for years to come.

John recorded five consecutive 30-save seasons from 1987 to 1991. His five-year total of 166 was the most in the NL during that period.

John led the league in saves in 1988, 1990, and 1994. He won the Fireman of the Year award each season.

Highlights

John holds the major-league record for career saves by a left-handed pitcher.

John pitched to 32 straight batters without allowing a hit in 1987. If he had been a starter, this would have added up to more than one complete-game no-hitter.

In 1988, the Reds called on John to save 42 games. He came through 39 times, for a remarkable save percentage of 92.8.

Reaching

John Franco is one of the most active players in the league when it comes to getting involved in a good cause. He gives his time to programs such as the Special Olympics, American Cancer Society, and the American Heart Association. John is also the team's best salesman, going out into the community during the off-season and creating new fans by giving clinics and playing ball with kids.

"Whatever I can do—if I have the time to do it—I'm always happy to help out."

John greets a new Mets fan. John is a tireless promoter of baseball to kids.

Out

John gives pitching tips at Father Flanagan's Boys Town in Brooklyn, New York.

Numbers

Name: John Anthony Franco

Born: September 17, 1960

Height: 5' 10"

Weight: 185 pounds

Uniform Number: 31

College: St. John's University

Year	Team	Games	Innings	ERA	Wins	Saves
1984	Cincinnati Reds	54	79.1	2.61	6	4
1985	Cincinnati Reds	67	99.0	2.18	12	12
1986	Cincinnati Reds	74	101.0	2.94	6	29
1987	Cincinnati Reds	68	82.0	2.52	8	32
1988	Cincinnati Reds	70	86.0	1.57	6	39*
1989	Cincinnati Reds	60	80.2	3.12	4	32
1990	New York Mets	55	67.2	2.53	5	33*
1991	New York Mets	52	55.1	2.93	5	30
1992	New York Mets	31	33.0	1.64	6	15
1993	New York Mets	35	36.1	5.20	4	10
1994	New York Mets	47	50.0	2.70	1	30*
1995	New York Mets	48	51.2	2.44	5	29
Totals		661	822.0	2.62	68	295

* Led League

What If...

When I signed my first pro contract, I was one of hundreds of good young pitchers in the minor leagues. What got me to the majors when so many others didn't make it? Hard work and commitment. I really believe that you can be anything you want to be if you work hard enough. Of course, in baseball, there is always the chance you could hurt yourself. Luckily, that's not much of a problem in other types of work. What would I have done if something like an arm injury had ended my career? I could definitely see myself in some sort of law-enforcement career, with the police or the FBI. I think the courses I took in college, and my interest in how people feel and how they think would have made me a success in that career."

Glossary

CONSECUTIVE several events that follow one after another

CONVERT to change something into something different

ACCESS the ability to obtain or make use of

AFFILIATE a connected branch of an organization

COMMODITY something or someone of great value; an asset; an advantage

COMPILE collect; gather; amass

PREDICT to guess what will happen in the future

REVEAL to bring out in the open; to show

SCHOLARSHIP money given to a student to help pay for schooling

VETERAN one who has a lot of experience

DISCO also called a "discotheque"; a dance club featuring disco music popular in the 1970s

DOMINANT the most powerful person or team

FLASH IN THE PAN one that appears promising but turns out to be disappointing or worthless

About The Author

Mark Stewart grew up in New York City in the 1960s and 1970s—when the Mets, Jets, and Knicks all had championship teams. As a child, Mark read everything about sports he could lay his hands on. Today, he is one of the busiest sportswriters around. Since 1990, he has written close to 500 sports stories for kids, including profiles on more than 200 athletes, past and present. A graduate of Duke University, Mark served as senior editor of *Racquet*, a national tennis magazine, and was managing editor of *Super News*, a sporting goods industry newspaper. He is the author of every Grolier All-Pro Biography.